AFFILIATE MARKETING 2023

2023

FOR BEGINNERS

HOW TO BE A UNIQUE AFFILIATE MARKETER

TABLE OF CONTENT

INTRODUCTION

Affiliate marketing has become a popular strategy for companies of all sizes to enhance their online presence and attract new clients. It helps marketers to use the audience and marketing knowledge of affiliates, while affiliates may earn cash by promoting items or services that correspond with their interests or speciality.

Affiliate marketing may be done in a number of ways, such as via blog articles, social media promotion, email marketing, and paid advertising. The key to success in affiliate marketing is to discover the proper affiliates that have a relevant audience and are enthusiastic about advertising your items, while also ensuring that your fee structure is appealing enough to entice them to sell your products over others.

CHAPTER ONE

Affiliate marketing is a sort of internet marketing where a firm (also known as the merchant or advertiser) compensates affiliates (also known as publishers or partners) for promoting their goods or services.

This is often done via an affiliate scheme, where the affiliate is given a unique URL or code to share with their audience. When a consumer clicks on the affiliate's link and makes a purchase or takes a specified action (such as filling out a lead form), the affiliate gets a commission on the transaction or lead.

Here are some crucial aspects to know about affiliate marketing:

Minimal risk for the merchant: As the merchant only pays a commission when a sale or lead is created, they don't have to spend money on advertising unless it results in a desired activity. This might make it a cost-effective strategy to market their goods or services.

Cost-effective for the affiliate: Affiliates don't have to develop or own any items, and may earn a percentage on purchases or leads created via their content. This may make it a fantastic option for bloggers, influencers, and content producers to monetize their online presence.

Improved visibility and reach for the merchant: Affiliates may promote the merchant's goods or services to their audience, which can assist to build brand recognition and bring more visitors to the merchant's website.

A win-win situation: Both the merchant and affiliate can gain from affiliate marketing, since the merchant can drive more sales and the affiliate can receive a commission on those transactions.

An internet marketing strategy called affiliate marketing pays companies or people (affiliates) a commission for each sale generated by a link they provided.

The merchant, the affiliate, and the customer are generally the three parties involved in the process. Although the affiliate is the individual who advertises the product or service to their audience via different marketing channels like websites, social media, or email marketing, the merchant (or advertiser) is the business that owns or sells the good or service.

For each purchase completed using their special affiliate link or referral code, affiliates get a commission. The product or service being marketed, as well as the affiliate program's rules, affect the commission rate. Although some systems charge a flat cost for each sale or lead produced, others charge a portion of the selling price.

Bloggers, social media influencers, and website owners that have a loyal following that respects their recommendations are big fans of affiliate marketing.

By advertising goods or services that meet the requirements and interests of their target market, it may be profitable to generate passive revenue.

In general, affiliate marketing is a win-win situation for all parties involved.

CHAPTER TWO

HERE ARE SOME ACTIONS YOU MAY TAKE IF YOU WANT TO START USING AFFILIATE MARKETING:

DECIDE ON A NICHE:

Decide on a particular passion or area of expertise that you wish to concentrate on. This may be everything from technology and gadgets to fashion and beauty to health and wellness. It's crucial to choose a niche that both the market and you are enthusiastic about.

Find affiliate programs that are appropriate for your niche by doing research on them. You may browse for specific affiliate programs from businesses you wish to promote online or search for affiliate networks.

JOIN AFFILIATE PROGRAMS:

After choosing the affiliate networks you wish to join, sign up and follow the on-screen instructions to get going. You could be asked to provide a few pieces of information about yourself, your website, and any social media profiles you have.

SELECTING ITEMS FOR PROMOTION:

Choose goods or services that fit your specialty and that you believe your target market would find appealing. Promotional items like banners and text links are often located on the affiliate program dashboard.

GENERATE CONTENT:

To produce material that advertises the goods or services you've selected, use your website, blog, social media accounts, or email list. Provide value to your audience by creating insightful and captivating content, and be sure to disclose your affiliate affiliation to your audience.

MONITOR YOUR PROGRESS:

To keep tabs on your clicks, sales, and commissions, use the reporting tools in the dashboard of your affiliate program. This will enable you to determine which goods and sales are most effective for you.

Keep in mind that affiliate marketing is a long-term tactic that demands tolerance, perseverance, and commitment. Developing a following and seeing results may take some time, but with the appropriate strategy, it may be a fruitful method to monetise your online presence.

CHAPTER THREE

HOW TO PICK A NICHE

Finding a particular area of interest or an issue that people need answers for, then advertising goods or services that meet that need, is the process of choosing a niche in affiliate marketing. The following steps will assist you in selecting a niche:

Determine your areas of interest and expertise: Start by coming up with a list of subjects you are educated or enthusiastic about. You will find it simpler to produce content and advertise goods in that area as a result.

 Research the market: To ascertain which themes are popular and have successful affiliate programs, use resources like Google Trends, Amazon Best Sellers, and other market research tools.

Analyze the amount of competition in your niche by counting the number of affiliates offering comparable goods and services. Search for niches where demand and competition are well balanced.

Think about profitability: Choose a market with high commission rates and chances for recurring revenue. This will increase the return on your labor.

Have a look at the affiliate programs: Search for affiliate programs that provide top-notch items, respectable commissions, and top-notch customer service. Verify the circumstances of each program to make sure they complement your objectives and tactics.

After you've settled on a niche, test it out and monitor your progress by marketing things. Analytical techniques may be used to evaluate your progress and, if necessary, modify your plans.

Keep in mind that picking an affiliate marketing specialty needs strategy, patience, and research. Take your time to choose the ideal specialty that aligns with your interests, abilities, and professional objectives.

CHAPTER FOUR

ADVANCED AFFILIATE STRATEGIES

Advanced affiliate tactics entail employing more advanced ways to boost the efficacy and profitability of your affiliate marketing operations. Here are some advanced affiliate methods to consider:

Utilize dynamic advertisements: Dynamic ads enable you to dynamically refresh your ad content with relevant items, graphics, and text depending on user activity and preferences. This may assist enhance engagement and conversions by giving customised content to each user.

Segment your audience: Segmenting your audience into multiple groups based on interests, demographics, and behaviors will help you offer more focused and relevant information to each group. This might boost the efficacy of your affiliate marketing efforts by offering the correct message to the right audience.

Provide special discounts: Providing unique bargains to your affiliate partners might incentivise them to market your items more aggressively. This may assist improve sales and generate more people to your site.

Employ retargeting: Retargeting enables you to target visitors who have already visited your site or interacted with your content. By employing retargeting advertisements, you may re-engage these people and remind them about your goods or services.

Optimize your landing pages: Your landing pages are important to the effectiveness of your affiliate marketing operations. Optimizing your landing pages for conversion will assist boost the possibility of people doing the intended action, whether that's making a purchase or signing up for a subscription.

Employ influencer marketing: Influencer marketing entails working with social media influencers to promote your goods or services to their following. This may be an efficient strategy to reach a bigger audience and enhance brand recognition.

Employ cross-channel promotions: Cross-channel promotions entail marketing your goods or services over numerous channels, such as email, social media, and paid advertising. This may assist boost your reach and attract more visitors to your site.

By adopting these advanced affiliate methods, you may boost the success of your affiliate marketing efforts and produce more sales and money for your company.

CHAPTER FIVE

HOW TO SELECT AFFILIATE PRODUCTS TO SELL

Choosing the correct affiliate items is vital for the success of your affiliate marketing activities. Here are some procedures to take when deciding which affiliate items to promote:

Identify your specialization: Start by determining your niche or area of expertise. Your specialty should be something you are enthusiastic about and have understanding on.

Research affiliate programs: Search for affiliate programs that are related to your expertise. You may start by searching on Google or affiliate networks.

Assess the product: After you have chosen an affiliate program that suits your niche, examine the product or service. Make sure it is a high-quality product that you would use yourself. You should also examine the product's demand, competition, and commission rates.

Verify the commission rate: Commission rates vary from program to program, so be careful to check the commission rate before advertising a product. Search for items with a high commission rate, but don't disregard smaller commission rates if the product is very relevant to your niche and has a solid conversion rate.

Verify the conversion rate: The conversion rate is the proportion of visitors who actually buy the product after clicking on your affiliate link. Search for items with a high conversion rate to guarantee that you make a significant revenue from your affiliate marketing efforts.

Examine the marketing materials: Search for affiliate programs that give marketing resources such as banners, product photos, and sales writing. This will make it easy for you to advertise the product efficiently.

Read reviews: See reviews from other affiliates who have advertised the product. This will give you an indication of how well the product converts and if it is worth advertising.

By following these methods, you may pick the ideal affiliate items that will help you create more cash and develop a successful affiliate marketing company.

CHAPTER SIX

HOW TO CREATE AN AUDIENCE AND MARKET THE PRODUCT AFFILIATE MARKETING

Developing an audience and marketing a product via affiliate marketing follows similar procedures as conventional marketing, with an emphasis on promoting the affiliate product. These are the measures you may take to establish an audience and advertise an affiliate product effectively:

Determine your target audience: In affiliate marketing, it's crucial to identify your target audience. Identify who your audience is and what they need. Consider criteria such as age, gender, location, hobbies, and requirements.

Research affiliate items: Search for affiliate products that correspond with your selected niche. You may locate affiliate programs on affiliate networks such as ShareASale, CJ Affiliate, and Amazon Associates.

Evaluate the product: Assess the affiliate product to verify it's a high-quality product that corresponds with your audience's demands. Consider aspects such as demand, competition, and commission rates.

Generate content: Develop material that resonates with your intended audience. It's crucial to deliver value to your audience by generating useful, entertaining, and relevant content. You may develop content in the form of blog entries, videos, social media postings, or email marketing campaigns.

Promote the affiliate product: Promote the affiliate product by adding affiliate links to your article. Be honest with your audience about your affiliate arrangement and ensure your promotions are ethical.

Create an email list: Develop an email list by delivering a lead magnet, like as a free e-book or course, in return for your audience's email address. You may then utilize your email list to advertise affiliate items and create a connection with your audience.

Interact with your audience: Connect with your audience by replying to comments, emails, and social media communications. This will help you form a connection with your audience and generate trust.

By following these methods, you may establish an audience and advertise affiliate items efficiently in affiliate marketing. Remember to emphasize delivering value to your audience and being upfront about your affiliate arrangement.

CHAPTER SEVEN

EFFECTIVE MODERN TOOLS AND STRATEGIES TO USE IN AFFILIATE MARKETING FOR BEGINNERS

If you're a newbie in affiliate marketing, there are various current tools and tactics that you may utilize to increase your marketing efforts. These are some of them:

Affiliate networks: Affiliate networks such as CJ Affiliate, and Amazon Associates offer a platform for affiliate marketers to identify and promote affiliate items. These networks provide a large selection of items and services to pick from and give a simplified method for affiliate marketing.

Social media marketing: Social media sites such as Facebook, Instagram, Twitter, and Pinterest are great marketing tools for affiliate marketers. You may utilize them to develop a brand, communicate with your audience, and promote your affiliate items.

Email marketing: Email marketing is a strong tool that enables you to interact with your audience directly. You may utilize it to market your affiliate items, create connections with your audience, and generate leads.

Content marketing: Content marketing entails providing useful and informative material that connects with your audience. You may generate blog entries, videos, infographics, and other sorts of material to attract and engage your audience and sell your affiliate items.

SEO: Search engine optimization (SEO) entails improving your website and content to rank better in search engine results pages. By employing targeted keywords, providing high-quality content, and developing backlinks, you may boost your website's exposure and attract more visitors.

Lead magnets: Lead magnets are free materials that you provide to your audience in return for their email addresses. Lead magnets may be e-books, courses, templates, or other unique materials that your audience might find beneficial. After you have their email addresses, you can utilize email marketing to advertise your affiliate items and create a connection with your audience.

By adopting these current tools and tactics, you may increase your affiliate marketing efforts and build your company as a novice.

CONCLUSION

Conclusion on becoming a unique affiliate

Being a distinctive affiliate involves a mix of elements such as originality, innovation, and a deep grasp of the industry and audience. To be successful as an affiliate, it's necessary to separate oneself from others in the same specialty or business. This may be done through delivering unique and useful material, building a strong personal brand, and cultivating a devoted and engaged audience.

In addition, creating connections with merchants and being choosy about the items or services you advertise may also help you stand out as a distinctive affiliate. It's crucial to concentrate on creating trust and credibility with your audience, since this may lead to long-term success and a sustainable revenue stream.

Eventually, being a distinctive affiliate demands a dedication to continual learning, testing, and reacting to changes in the market and audience preferences. By being ahead of the curve and giving unique value to your audience, you may separate yourself from competitors and achieve success as an affiliate marketer.

www.ingramcontent.com/pod-product-compliance
Lightning Source LLC
Chambersburg PA
CBHW070523220526
45467CB00002B/813